Seasons

Summer

Patricia Whitehouse

Heinemann Library
Chicago, Illinois

Designed by Sue Emerson, Heinemann Library
Printed and bound in the U.S.A. by Lake Book

07 06 05 04
10 9 8 7 6 5 4 3

Library of Congress Cataloging-in-Publication Data
Whitehouse, Patricia, 1958–
    Summer / Patricia Whitehouse.
       v. cm. — (Seasons)
Includes index.
Contents: What are seasons?—What is the weather like in summer?—What do you wear in summer?—What can you see in summer?—What can you smell in summer?—What can you hear in summer?—What can you taste in summer?—What special things can you do in summer?
    ISBN: 1-58810-891-0 (HC), 1-40340-542-5 (Pbk.)
    1. Summer—Juvenile literature. [1. Summer.] I. Title. II. Seasons (Heinemann Library)
    QB637.6 .W48 2003
    508.2—dc21

6802   2002001165

Acknowledgments
The author and publishers are grateful to the following for permission to reproduce copyright material:
pp. 4, 5 J. A. Kraulis/Masterfile; p. 6 Richard Shock/Stone/Getty Images; p. 7 J. P. Fruchet/FPG International; p. 8 Gibson Stock Photography; p. 9L Michael Newman/PhotoEdit; p. 9R Jack Ballard/Visuals Unlimited; p. 10L BananaStock, Ltd./PictureQuest; p. 10R Photo Researchers, Inc.; p. 11 E. Dygas/PhotoDisc; p. 12 Nance S. Trueworthy/Stock Boston; p. 13L Frank Oberle/Stone/Getty Images; p. 13R Ralph A. Clevenger/Corbis; p. 14 Jeff Greenberg/Visuals Unlimited; p. 15L Mark E. Gibson/Visuals Unlimited; p. 15R Phyllis Picardi/Stock Boston; p. 16L Don Spiro/Stone/Getty Images; p. 16R David Young-Wolff/Photo Edit; p. 17 Eyewire Collection; p. 18L Stephen McBrady/Photo Edit; p. 18R Brian Drake/West Stock Inc.; p. 19L Sandy Clark/Index Stock Imagery, Inc.; p. 19R Comstock Images; p. 20 Andrew McCaul/The Image Bank/Getty Images; p. 21L Susie Leavines/Mira.com; p. 21R Gibson Stock Photography; p. 22 (row 1, L-R) Michael Newman/PhotoEdit, Nance S. Trueworthy/Stock Boston; p. 22 (row 2, L-R) Mark E. Gibson/Visuals Unlimited, Don Spiro/Stone/Getty Images; p. 22 (row 3) Kent Dufault/Index Stock Imagery, Inc./PictureQuest; p. 23 (row 1, L-R) Mark Cassino/BananaStock, Ltd./PictureQuest, C Squared Studios/PhotoDisc; p. 23 (row 2, L-R) Susie Leavines/Mira.com, Ryan McVay/PhotoDisc, Mark E. Gibson/Visuals Unlimited; p. 23 (row 3, L-R) C Squared Studios/PhotoDisc/Picture Desk, Eyewire Collection; p. 23 (row 4, L-R) Image State, Siede Preis/PhotoDisc

Cover photograph by David Schmidt/Masterfile
Photo research by Scott Braut

Every effort has been made to contact copyright holders of any material reproduced in this book. Any omissions will be rectified in subsequent printings if notice is given to the publisher.

Special thanks to our advisory panel for their help in the preparation of this book:

Eileen Day, Preschool Teacher
Chicago, IL

Ellen Dolmetsch, MLS
Wilmington, DE

Kathleen Gilbert,
Second Grade Teacher
Austin, TX

Sandra Gilbert,
Library Media Specialist
Houston, TX

Angela Leeper,
Educational Consultant
North Carolina Department
of Public Instruction
Raleigh, NC

Pam McDonald,
Reading Teacher
Winter Springs, FL

Melinda Murphy,
Library Media Specialist
Houston, TX

Some words are shown in bold, **like this.**
You can find them in the picture glossary on page 23.

Contents

What Is Summer?

| summer | fall |

Summer is a season.

There are four seasons in a year.

winter	spring

In most places, each season brings new things to see and do.

What Is the Weather Like in Summer?

Summer is the hottest season.

The days and nights are warm.

Most summer days are sunny.

But there are rainy days, too.

What Do You Wear in Summer?

You can wear shorts and T-shirts.

You can wear swimsuits
and **sandals.**

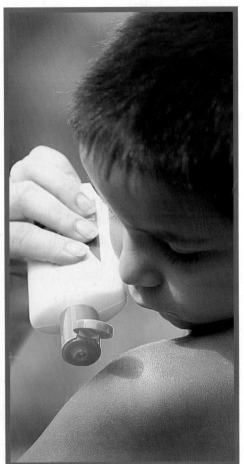

Sunglasses keep your eyes safe from the sun.

Sunscreen keeps your skin from getting burned by the sun.

What Can You Feel in Summer?

You can feel hot **sand** on your toes.

You can feel cool water on your skin.

You can feel the sun on your face.

You can feel soft grass tickling your back.

What Can You See in Summer?

You can see fruits and vegetables growing in gardens.

You can see green leaves on the trees.

You can see animals keeping cool.

You can see butterflies flying.

What Can You Smell in Summer?

You can smell smoke from **grills.**

You can smell food cooking outside.

You can smell hot **tar** on the streets.

You can smell freshly cut grass.

What Can You Hear in Summer?

You can hear a baseball game.

You can hear the bells on the ice cream truck.

You can hear **tractors** in the fields.

You can hear **sprinklers** spraying water.

What Can You Taste in Summer?

You can taste juicy hamburgers.

You can taste sweet watermelon.

You can taste **lemonade.**

You can taste creamy ice cream.

What Special Things Can You Do in Summer?

You can catch **fireflies**.

Later, you can let them go!

You can go to a street fair.

You can see **fireworks** on the Fourth of July.

Quiz

What can you see in the summer?

Picture Glossary

firefly
page 20

sand
page 10

sunscreen
page 9

fireworks
page 21

sandals
page 8

tar
page 15

grill
page 14

sprinkler
page 17

tractor
page 17

lemonade
page 19

sunglasses
page 9

Note to Parents and Teachers

Reading for information is an important part of a child's literacy development. Learning begins with a question about something. Help children think of themselves as investigators and researchers by encouraging their questions about the world around them. Each chapter in this book begins with a question. Read the question together. Look at the pictures. Talk about what you think the answer might be. Then read the text to find out if your predictions were correct. Think of other questions you could ask about the topic, and discuss where you might find the answers. Assist children in using the picture glossary and the index to practice new vocabulary and research skills.

Index